Deeper Than Dentistry

My Journey From Death's Door to Marketplace Ministry

Deeper Than Dentistry

MY JOURNEY FROM DEATH'S DOOR TO MARKETPLACE MINISTRY

GARY BETHEA

Design Grade Design and Adeline Media, London

First print December 2020

CONTENTS

A NOTE FROM THE AUTHOR

n life, we face adversity, trials, and various difficult circumstances. In the midst of these moments, we tend to ask questions. Why is this happening? What am I to do? How long will this last? These are questions for which we desire answers. Over the years, I come to realize that even if we receive the answers, the answers are not what is most needed. What is most needed is God's presence. Being still and knowing that God is with you is enough. I want to thank God for being with me not only during my mountain experiences (highs) but also during my valley experiences (lows).

"When you go through deep waters, I will be with you.
When you go through rivers of difficulty, you will not drown.
When you walk through the fire of oppression, you will not be
burned up; the flames will not consume you."

Isaiah 43:2

PROLOGUE

Never thought I'd die this early in life. How did I let myself get here? Surely, God doesn't want to hear from me now. Is heaven out of reach for me?

That terrifying thought tortured my mind as I lay in the dark car trunk—beaten, bloodied, bruised, bound with tape... and bound for a horrible fate.

Death wouldn't even be the worst part. Death would be a relief, if not for the unimaginable punishment that would follow: eternal darkness and torment.

At sixteen years old, I was too young to die, but my poor choices had doomed me and my three friends. I had done thoughtless, stupid, sinful things. And now I was paying the price.

My actions had brought me face to face with demons, and I would soon meet the devil himself.

I began praying as I'd never prayed before. "God, I am sorry for what I have done. Is there any way you can forgive me?"

Unexpectedly, peace settled over me. And I fell asleep.

1

LIFE IN A SMALL TOWN

Growing up in Bennettsville, South Carolina, I never would have dreamed that I'd be where I am today. Bennettsville, near the South Carolina-North Carolina state line, is the biggest city and county seat of Marlboro County, but it's a small town where not a lot goes on. According to the 2010 census, Bennettsville's

The Marlboro County Courthouse located in downtown Bennettsville.

population was 9,069; the county's 28,933. The county has one high school. Walmart didn't arrive until 2012.

I am the youngest of three born into the household of Otis and Linda Bethea. Otis Jr. was born in 1979; Sherry in 1981; I came along in 1984. My dad was the oldest of eight children, my mother the youngest of eleven. He's four years older than she is.

We were a blue-collar family. My dad worked twelve hours a day at Mohawk Carpet, with his days off rotating week to week. He worked that job for 40 years, from the time he graduated from high school.

My mother worked for the Department of Social Services. Her job put her in a position to know a lot of people, but privacy rules kept her from sharing who and what she knew. That gave her a bit of mystique.

My parents didn't have the perfect marriage, but they gave us a two-parent home and did the best they could. Seeing how hard they worked instilled a strong work ethic early on in us kids.

My mother and father got married March 19, 1977.

At school, I regularly got in trouble—not for fighting or major offenses, but for little things like talking in class. Truth is, I sometimes swallowed my pride to avoid fights. While that may have made me less respected as a "tough guy," it kept me from getting suspended or, worse, disappointing my mom. I always made good grades, although I didn't give them much thought in elementary or middle school. School was mostly about playing football at recess and hanging with friends.

***

There wasn't much for a kid to do in Bennettsville. The two closest malls were in Florence, South Carolina, 30-some miles away, and Fayetteville, North Carolina, 60 miles away. There was no community pool for everyone. The local pool was more like a country club, not for my friends and me. When we wanted to go swimming, my dad would drive us to a place called South of the Border in Dillon, 25 or 30 miles away.

Summers were mostly spent running around the neighborhood playing tag or chase. These were innocent times, though rough elements and dangers lurked nearby. My parents did their best to make sure we didn't fall prey to alcohol and drugs, perils that lured some of my peers as early as middle school.

The D.A.R.E. (Drug Abuse Resistance Education) program that visited schools was probably the single most important influence in keeping me away from harmful substances. "D.A.R.E. to keep kids off drugs" was the slogan, and it worked on me. Those cartoonish videos showing zombie-like people on drugs really frightened me. Later, when I saw friends doing drugs, I became angry.

On one occasion, I was at my house with a childhood friend and two cousins, one of whom was visiting from New York, where life was a lot faster. The New York cousin inquired about scoring some marijuana. I was mad that my friend was actually able to get it. Next thing I knew, the three of them were smoking weed in my backyard. I protested furiously: "Man, what in the world are y'all doing?"

In my experience, weed made people not care about school or anything. Peer pressure or not, this was something I would never do. I have lost friends to the drug lifestyle. Now, as a father, I pray that when my kids get older, they take on a mindset of settled obedience. That's when you know there are certain things you'll never do, under any circumstances. We can't have partial obedience; it needs to be settled obedience. Many of us have willing obedience, but then things happen, and we may compromise. Settled obedience is intentional. Daniel in the Old Testament is a good example. He purposed in his heart that he wouldn't defile himself. When he and his friends got sent to Babylon, they were expected to eat and drink the royal food and wine and to bow down to King Nebuchadnezzar's golden statue. But they refused to do so, even at the risk of their lives.

Settled obedience means staying true to what you know

you will and will not do. It's settled before it becomes an issue. For me, drugs weren't something to leave to chance or temptation. I also credit my parents for my feelings about drugs. Drinking and smoking and drug use just didn't go on in our house.

***

Although my brother and sister are five and three years older than me, we were pretty close growing up. My dad worked 8:00 a.m. to 8:00 p.m., and my mother worked 8 to 5, so in the summertime when she left for work, on the days when we didn't go to our grandparents' house, she'd tell us not to go outside.

3rd grade picture day.

Of course, we kids wouldn't stay inside. There was too much going on in the neighborhood! We'd wake up about 10:00 a.m., and my brother would sometimes make breakfast. Then we'd go outside and play until just before Mama came home on her lunch break. At 12:40, we'd run in the house and act as if we'd been there the whole time. She'd fix lunch, go back to work at 2:00, and by 2:15, we'd be back outside playing. At 4:40, we'd run back in.

Now and then, Mama would come home unexpectedly to check on us, and she'd catch us outside. We'd get a spanking, but that didn't stop us from doing it again.

Growing up in a small town made you closer to people. There wasn't much to do but spend time with people. In Bennettsville, you enjoy people because you don't really have places to go.

***

As a kid, you can't wait to grow up, leave town, go off and do stuff, and see the world. But looking back, I realize we had a lot of fun. Until the age of ten or twelve, you're innocent. My friends and I spent most of our free time playing outside, riding bikes, and running around the neighborhood.

There were few fences. You could run through someone's backyard and be on the next block. Everybody was close. Most parents had at least three kids, so my siblings and I all had plenty of friends our age. We played baseball in the street and used mailboxes as bases. We played football and basketball in my backyard.

My home the first 18 years of my life. This picture was taken in 2001.

These days, I live in a really nice neighborhood, but people stay in their houses. Where I grew up wasn't the nicest neighborhood, but it was alive. Everybody was always outside.

Having an older brother and sister looking out for me probably kept me from being a follower when I got to school. They gave good counsel. Otis was always telling me, "Fix your shirt" or "Quit chewing on your shirt." He made sure I didn't walk around looking a mess. Sherry also did her part.

My cousin Romeon has been a close friend since we were in diapers. He was born in March 1984; I came along in July. With all my cousins and neighborhood friends, I didn't have to try to fit in at school. That helped me not become a follower.

***

Church was a regular part of my upbringing. Our mom took us kids to Shiloh Baptist Church. Our dad went to Mount Zion Baptist. We all went to Mount Zion until I was two or three, then my mom started taking us kids to Shiloh, the church she grew up in. It's still my hometown church, and I visit whenever I'm in Bennettsville for a weekend.

We had to be there every Sunday morning—no ifs, ands, or buts. Mama taught Sunday school, so we had to go to be there for that, too. If we acted sick so we could stay home, we couldn't go anywhere the rest of the day.

Sunday school was where I learned a lot about the Bible: Jonah and the whale, David and Goliath, Samson and Delilah. I didn't start paying attention to the pastor and his sermon until maybe sixth grade. My church friends and I would sit in the back of the church and play tic-tac-toe.

My brother at 21 and my sister at 19. They have always looked after me.

2

NOT TRYING TOO HARD

My friends were in mostly separate groups: cousins, neighborhood playmates, school friends, church friends. My same-age cousins were the closest, because on weekends we'd all play at our grandparents' house. Cousin Romeon fit into two groups; though we rarely had a class together, we got together at recess. Almost every weekend, we spent the night at one of our houses. During the summer, we might do that three nights a week.

My school friends were mostly good kids. My neighborhood friends, the ones I rode the school bus with, were a little rougher. As for the church friends, by the time I got to high school, I'd see them around, and we were cool with each other, but we didn't hang out.

I didn't get serious about grades until eleventh grade, though I started paying a little more attention in middle school after making the honor roll and getting a few awards. But mostly I was preoccupied with other pursuits.

I always loved football and as a kid dreamed of going to

the NFL. I was short but fast and quick. When we played football during recess in elementary and middle school, I was one of the fastest kids on the field. I played tailback on offense and cornerback on defense. In sixth grade, on the Mighty Mikes football team, one day my coaches noticed how fast I was doing some drills. They put me in a game, and I scored a touchdown the first time I ran the ball. For the rest of the season, I was the starting running back. Then, in seventh and eighth grades, you had to try out, and both years I made the team.

By the time I got to real football in high school, competition was steep, with one school serving the whole county. My playground game never really translated into organized ball. I was too small to catch the coaches' attention. To be honest, I was a little afraid once we put pads on, and I went onto the field to get hit by much bigger kids. Before the game, the butterflies in my stomach were almost overwhelming, though I would be fine when I actually got in a game. But I never really got a chance to prove myself.

By high school, football was more like a job, requiring a lot of practice and lifting weights, and I was embarrassed that I couldn't lift as much as the others. My NFL dream ended around tenth grade, and by eleventh grade, I had stopped playing.

***

When I got to Marlboro County High School, I was still getting good grades without too much effort. My focus was on friendships, playing football, and the girls I was starting to notice.

In tenth grade, I received a letter inviting me to go off to the South Carolina Governor's School for Science and Mathematics for my junior and senior years. My friend Lance, whom I'd known since second grade, decided to attend the school, 25 to 30 minutes away in Hartsville. Students pretty much stayed there, like going away to college. I chose to remain with my other friends at Marlboro County High.

Toward the end of eleventh grade, we learned who the junior marshals were. Those who maintained a certain GPA graduated with honors and a gold strip around their neck. Juniors on track to graduate with honors were called junior marshals, and they served as ushers when the seniors graduated.

One day, I realized I wasn't a junior marshal.

People considered me smart, and I could make an A if I really tried, but I was OK with a B or C. I was too distracted by other stuff to worry about grades. But when my guidance counselor told me I wasn't a junior marshal, it stung. I felt just as smart as the junior marshals, who also seemed surprised that I hadn't made the cut. I was just shy of the required 3.5 GPA, and that shortcoming lit a fire inside me.

***

Social life, especially girls, was a major aspect of high school for me. I never felt like the most handsome guy, I was shorter than most of my friends, and I didn't have muscles like some of my peers. But one thing I could control was how I dressed, so that's where I distinguished myself. People came to know me for being really "fly." When shopping for school clothes, I did the best with the money my parents gave me—I had a knack for finding the right threads and wearing them the right way. For senior superlatives, I was voted "Best Dressed."

I was a junior when I started talking to the girl who would become my high school sweetheart. While no longer playing sports—partly because I just couldn't let her see me sitting on the sidelines—I appreciated that Marlboro County High was known for championships. During my four years there, we won a title every year except my sophomore year. When I was in ninth grade, the Bulldogs football team went 15–0 and won the state title. In tenth grade, we lost in the basketball championship. In eleventh grade, we won it all in basketball, and in twelfth grade, we again went 15–0 in football and were champions.

My future high school sweetheart and I started talking at the state basketball championship game on March 9, 2001. Less than two months later, just as we were starting to get serious, my life was turned upside down.

***

It was a weird and eventful time with a lot of energy in the air. My school had just won the state championship, I had just started dating this girl, and the end of school was nearing. I also had been invited to attend the National

My junior year of High School.

Youth Leadership Forum on Medicine. I wanted to attend this conference, set for July in Chicago, but it cost $2,000, and my family didn't have that kind of money. So my mom started raising money through our church. She even sent letters to other churches. Lo and behold, they ended up collecting enough money, and I had to walk down front before the congregation one Sunday and receive this big offering.

I hadn't decided on a career in medicine, though I'd thought it might be cool to be a doctor—or a lawyer, for that matter. But as a sixteen-year-old junior who had never ventured to the Midwest, I relished the opportunity to go to Chicago and maybe learn a little about medicine in the process.

3

SAVING GRACE

On the day that changed my life forever, I was supposed to have been in Hartsville, South Carolina, hanging with my friend Lance at Governor's School. We didn't have cell phones, so I emailed him to say I was thinking of coming up to play some hoops. But then I decided to go in another direction.

It was April 28, 2001, a Saturday near the end of my junior year of high school. My sister had let me borrow her car, a purple Honda with chrome rims and purple lights underneath it. With me were my neighbor and childhood friend, Quan, my cousin Romeon, and Jamarcus, whom we called Kiki. Instead of going to Governor's School, we went to hang with some of my cousins and their friends in the small town of Laurel Hill, in Scotland County, North Carolina.

After leaving my cousins' house to head home, we stopped for a bite in nearby Laurinburg at a drive-through restaurant stand called Central Park. That's when four girls pulled up next to us and invited us to a party. Opportunity had fallen into our laps!

The girls, who were easy on the eyes and seemed a little older, said they had to go by their apartment first, so we followed them. In my excitement, I wasn't thinking too much about my girlfriend, who happened to be a first cousin to Romeon's girlfriend. When we got there, my friends climbed out of the car, the girls got out of theirs, and I asked one of them to hop into my sister's Honda with me. I preferred to be alone with her rather than go into the apartment with everybody else. We drove to a nearby park and were in the car talking, getting to know each other, when the police pulled up and told us to leave. It was around 10:30 p.m., so we returned to the apartment. In hindsight, this girl played her part really well.

Upon opening the door to the apartment, I saw my friends sitting side by side on a couch in the living room. Suddenly the door closed behind me, and I felt something against the back of my head. I turned and found myself staring down the barrel of a sawed-off shotgun!

It was surreal, like a movie, and I've never felt more frightened. My sister's car keys were snatched from me, and while one guy held the gun to my head, another emptied my pockets. I had a wallet but no money. When they took the car keys, I stammered, "It's my sister's car." That didn't seem to matter. They kept asking me where my money was.

Our kidnappers forced me into a chair next to the couch.

Glancing around the room, I saw several rough-looking guys plus the four girls. A tall guy they called T-Bone was in charge. Everything seemed to move in slow motion. The sawed-off shotgun remained pointed at me.

Looking back, I recall one comical detail amid all the seriousness. The cigarette Quan had been smoking was just one long ash. He was so frozen he apparently hadn't taken a drag since they entered the apartment and found themselves in a predicament.

My friends later told me that as soon as they entered the apartment, these guys came out with guns and backed them onto the couch. A little later, as I approached the front door, the guy with the shotgun stood behind it and waited.

Now, after they had robbed us of what little we had, our kidnappers moved Quan, Romeon, and me to the kitchen and tied us up with tape. Kiki was on crutches, so they left him on the couch.

Even today, I feel as if I was dealing with demons in human form that night. Yet they apparently had sympathy for Kiki, who told them a sob story about hurting his ankle during a fight with Romeon a couple of weeks earlier. That injury and a lie about a close relative dying saved him from a lot of pain that night. He sat there, alone and unbothered, on the couch in the living room while we went through hours of torture in the kitchen.

By the time we were tied up, it was at least 11:00 p.m., maybe midnight. We were tied up in three chairs at a round kitchen table. I was in the chair closest to the hallway. Quan was to my right, in front of the counter and sink, and Romeon was straight across the table from me. To my left stood our kidnappers.

The interrogation shifted from "Where's your money?" to "What are you all doing in Laurinburg?" They had looked at our driver's licenses and seen we were from Bennettsville. "You shouldn't even be here!" they hissed. Though they had sent the girls to set us up—to set somebody up, at least—now they acted mad that we had dared to come to their town and talk to their girls.

For the next four hours or so, they used our faces as punching bags while the girls watched. We could do nothing to defend ourselves. Because of where I was sitting, I was the most convenient target and got the worst of it. At one point, my chair toppled over, and I fell with it, my face slamming into the floor. They picked me back up and continued their attack.

About two hours into the ordeal, I just knew they were going to kill us. Quan's and Romeon's faces were bruised and swollen. Quan had long hair in braids, almost like dreadlocks. They cut part of his braids, and at one point they set his hair on fire but quickly put it out. They relentlessly taunted, cursed, and beat us, laughing and acting crazy.

Through it all, one song played on repeat. It was rapper Biggie Smalls, aka, The Notorious B.I.G., rapping "Somebody's Gotta Die." Over and over, we heard Biggie, who had been killed in a drive-by shooting in Los Angeles in 1997, intoning: *somebody gotta die. If I go, you gotta go. Somebody gotta die…*

Every now and then, T-Bone would hit us, but he mainly orchestrated the assault. They kept saying: "Why are you all up here? You shouldn't even be up here. You thought you were going to talk to our girls!" My face was almost numb, and I could only guess what it looked like. I had started silently asking God: *can I go ahead and die?* I saw no way we were leaving that apartment alive. I couldn't see out of one eye at all, it was so swollen.

Eventually, our kidnappers untied Romeon from the chair and took him out the back door. I heard a car start up and leave. My heart sank. I was sure they had taken him off to kill him. In a while, a couple of guys returned. They took Quan, still tied up, and Kiki, on crutches, out the back door, saving me for last. As they dragged me out, I saw an image that remains vividly etched into my mind. They backed my sister's car up to the rear of the apartment. Quan and Kiki were in the back seat, and the trunk was open. "Get the (blank) in the trunk," I was told. They threw me in.

I had always been afraid of drowning, not being able to breathe. I couldn't think of a more horrible way to die. Now I had to face that possibility. When they put me in the trunk, arms tied behind my back, and shut it, everything was pitch dark. Romeon was already dead, I feared, and we were next. They were going to dump my sister's car in the lake with Quan, Kiki, and me in it.

In addition to being consumed by fear and confusion, I was overwhelmed by guilt and beating myself up. I had gotten myself and my friends into this jam. I had let my sister's car get stolen. My parents were going to suffer the pain of losing their son because he'd been chasing girls. I felt like the biggest sinner in the world, and I was going to hell!

I also remembered: *man, I'm supposed to go to Chicago in two months!*

My church had raised all this money to send me to this medical conference that I would never attend. I wondered what all the people who were proud of me would think about me now. My girlfriend, my parents, and lots of others would be crushed when they found out I was dead.

Those thoughts were haunting me during that ride, which was probably 30 to 45 minutes. That feels like forever when you're tied up in the dark in a trunk.

In the midst of my confusion and fear, I started praying. It was the most sincere prayer, maybe the first sincere prayer, I'd ever offered up in my life:

"God, I know I've sinned. Just know, before I die, that I'm sorry. Is there any way you can forgive me?" I added that if He got me out of this, I would live for Him and never get in another situation like this.

***

I was baptized at nine years old. I made a public profession of faith, stood in front of the church, and was asked, "Do you believe that Jesus Christ died for your sins?" I said, "Yes" and believed it. After I got baptized, the feeling was, "Now you've got to try to be perfect." To a nine year old, the understanding of who Christ is and what He came to do was not very deep. I was saved, but I didn't truly understand what Christ had done for me and how I was supposed to apply that to my actual life.

Now, at age sixteen and facing death, the reality of Christ's sacrifice for my sins fell on me like an epiphany—or a ton of bricks. My understanding became crystal clear. It was like an inner voice telling me: *listen, Gary, I came here for you! Even though you did wrong, this doesn't send you to hell. I love you so much that I came to Earth and died to save you from ALL your sins.* During that conversation, I went from being afraid to having peace. I was ready to die. I felt like, *OK, I can come home now.* I felt a peace come over me.

I felt so at peace that I went to sleep in the trunk of that car.

***

When the car stopped, I awoke to the sounds of crickets. Nature. The trunk popped open, and I was pulled out of the trunk.

We were in the middle of nowhere. The headlights and taillights had been cut off, and I couldn't see a thing. Quan and Kiki had been dragged out of the back seat. Our kidnappers warned us: "You all better not say a (blankyblanking) word to nobody about this." Then one of them hit me, again, so hard that I felt as if my jaw had been broken. I fell to the ground and rolled down the drop-off on the side of the road.

Another set of headlights appeared. A car had been following us. The two bad guys hopped into that car and it drove off, leaving us standing there, stranded on a country road, next to my sister's car without its keys.

We freed ourselves from the tape that bound us, and my friends helped me to my feet. We started walking down the pitch-dark road, still in shock. When we saw lights approaching again, we scurried into the woods. The car kept coming and going, back and forth. We kept traveling through the woods at the side of the road.

We walked fifteen or twenty minutes before coming to lights and houses. It was about 3:00 a.m. We knocked on a door, and somebody opened it. We asked them to call the police.

When the police showed up, Romeon was with them—alive! Our captors had taken him to a different place than where they'd dropped us; he recognized it and ran for help.

The police took us to the hospital, where the doctors or technicians slid me into a machine (which was a little too much like the car trunk I'd just gotten out of)! They determined I had no broken bones, brain damage, or serious internal injuries, so it was off to the police station. Before long, my parents and my friends' parents arrived.

When my mom and dad saw my face, I could see their pain.

The police took my picture, and I didn't recognize myself. My left eye was red and swollen, my nose was bleeding, my lips were busted, and my cheek was bruised and swollen. (I underwent surgery for a burst eardrum a few days later, which is probably the worst pain I've ever endured. It didn't feel like the surgeon gave me anesthesia.)

Thank God, I still had all my teeth!

***

Despite our kidnappers' warning, we told the police what happened and showed them the apartment. The long, dark night ended with me back at home and going to bed, but not before studying my face in the mirror. I couldn't believe what I looked like, but I was grateful to be alive and home.

When I awoke in the morning, I heard my mom trying to prepare my brother for what I looked like. Otis, then 21, was working nights at the prison. Although he was doing honest work and not into the street life of drugs and guns like a lot of guys on our block, he had a temper and feared nobody. Mama knew that when Otis saw my condition, he would want to go do something. When he did see me, I saw hurt and anger on his face. He went outside, and I heard him and his friends talking about what happened and making plans.

I didn't leave the house for close to two weeks.

Tension was in the air. The story about the kidnapping

in The Laurinburg Exchange inflamed the natural rivalry between Marlboro County, South Carolina, and Scotland County, North Carolina. The police said anybody from Bennettsville caught in that part of Laurinburg would go to jail, no questions asked. Now, twenty years later, I can say that my brother and some of his friends did go up to Laurinburg, ready to do something. Thank God they didn't get a chance to hurt anyone.

Six of our kidnappers were arrested the Monday after the incident, and their colleagues eventually ended up behind bars. Tensions carried over into the next football season that fall, and extra police had to staff the Marlboro County-Scotland County football game.

**

The Old Testament book of Genesis tells the story of Joseph, one of twelve sons of Jacob. Their father loved Joseph more than the others and gave him a coat of many colors. His brothers became so jealous that one day, they sold him into slavery, telling their father that wild animals had killed him. Joseph was taken to Egypt, where he was made an overseer of the house of Potiphar, one of Pharaoh's officers. Potiphar's wife tried unsuccessfully to seduce Joseph and then falsely claimed he had tried to rape her. He was imprisoned.

But God was with Joseph while he was in prison. Joseph had a gift for interpreting dreams, and he correctly interpreted the dreams that were troubling Pharaoh.

Pharaoh responded by making Joseph his second in command over all Egypt.

Then a famine struck the land, and Jacob sent his sons to Egypt to buy grain, not realizing they would have to buy it from Joseph. The brothers soon came face to face with the one they had sold into slavery, but they didn't recognize him. When he finally revealed himself to them, they feared for their lives, but he tearfully embraced them in forgiveness. He told them, in Genesis 50:20, "You intended to harm me, but God intended it for good to accomplish what is now being done, the saving of many lives."

A lot of people talk about 20/20 vision, but I prefer 50:20 vision. 50/20 vision is the ability to see God working in a situation. That philosophy applies to what happened to me that night in Laurinburg when I thought I was going to die. The incident was a life-changing event, and God has used it for good.

Because of this, instead of trying to get even with the people who did me wrong, my focus turned to getting even with the people who did me right. It's human nature to want to retaliate, and some of my friends wanted to do so. I told them, if you do that, you'll find yourself in jail. Besides, vengeance is for God, not humans.

On the other hand, I did have some "settling up" to do. A lot of people had raised money for me to attend the medical conference in Chicago, and I know I disappointed them with my actions. So my mindset after the kidnapping was that the law and the Lord would deal with the people who did me wrong. I wanted to get even, to make amends, with the people who had looked out for me, raised money for me, and rooted for me.

I prayed, "God, if you get me out of this, I'm going to live for you," and He gave me more time. Since then, He has richly blessed me. I feel an obligation to honor that promise by giving God the glory for everything I do henceforth. I'm being allowed to shine so I can give Him the credit.

Sitting in my sister's 1998 Honda Accord at age 16. This is the same car that I was placed in the trunk of the night of the kidnapping.

THE LAURINBURG

EXCHANGE

TUESDAY,
MAY 1, 2001

PUBLISHED MONDAY
THROUGH FRIDAY
87TH EDITION
119TH YEAR

50 CENTS ESTABLISHED 1882 1 SECTION, 10 PAGES

Testimony begins in Hatcher murder trial
•PAGE 2

Estimates show that tax collections won't help state budget shortfall
•PAGE 2

Conference champs
SHS GOLF TAKES TITLE
SPORTS•PAGE 5

OPINION
•PAGE 4

Drug sentences
Raspberry is at it again

Cruising leads to robbery, kidnapping for S.C. teens

BY KEVIN DEGON
EDITOR

Laurinburg police arrested six people Monday and are looking for three more in connection with the robbery and kidnapping of four South Carolina teenagers who were apparently lured to a Scotland Manor apartment by four women and robbed early Sunday.

Police are still looking for three more men who

Our story was on the front page of the newspaper which came out a few days after the kidnapping. It did not take long for the news to spread.

4

FINISHING STRONG

still felt embarrassed about the kidnapping because the newspaper story revealed that, although we had been set up, it happened because we were doing something we had no business doing.

It was nearly three weeks before I returned to school. My face was so messed up, I was afraid to go back. Though I had been through quite an ordeal, I couldn't count on my classmates to treat the situation with the gravity it deserved. As a high school student, you worry about people making jokes at your expense, and I didn't want to be an easy target. When I did go back, the swelling had gone down, but I still had a black eye.

My face wasn't all I was worried about. I was concerned about how my girlfriend would react when she learned the facts. But she didn't even ask how we had gotten into that situation. She just seemed sad and sorry. We continued to date until near the end of my freshman year of college.

When it came to the judgment of my peers, I was more

or less on my own. I was the only one of the victims still attending Marlboro County High. By now, I was driving to school. Previously, I chose to ride the bus instead of having my parents take me. When you rode the bus, you rode with your neighborhood. You'd get off the bus and walk in with your block. The bell rang, and you went to class. There's strength in numbers. When you drove to school, you walked in on your own. I didn't want everybody to see me and start asking questions. So I sneaked in a side door and through the empty halls so I could already be in class before everybody else got there.

Rumors were already going around town. One story was that our kidnappers had made us strip naked. I was livid when I heard that. Romeon, being more hot tempered than I was, got in a fight with the guy he'd heard spreading that rumor.

My first day back at school, a girl in my keyboarding class walked up and said, "You look bad." That was true, but I saw no need to point out the obvious. I've never forgotten that.

***

Outside the physical damage, which soon healed, the kidnapping altered my awareness. Anybody could be telling me a story. Any girl I talked to could be lying. When I started college a little over a year later, I'd be wary about going to a girl's dorm. The other side of the equation was, even around kids who thought they were tough, my attitude had become:

"I can't fear anybody or anything because I've been through the worst." The incident had drawn me close enough to God to realize that a person can never kill the soul. Why should I be afraid of people?

I became a better person. I didn't become an instant saint, but the seed was planted. I was much more aware of my mortality. As a young person, you feel invincible until something like that happens. But the moment I looked down the barrel of that sawed-off shotgun, I realized how bad people can be. My nature has always been to think that although people do bad things, they're basically good. But the fact is that, in our flesh, even the best of us are bad. We're just saved by grace, if we believe in Christ. Instead of asking why bad stuff happens to good people, we should wonder why God allows good stuff to happen to us, knowing we don't deserve it.

The incident put me in a position to see humans for what they really are: a fallen people. That chilling night in Laurinburg was my first chance to be around people who just really didn't care. That night, it was as if I had met straight-up evil.

***

Having survived my dark night of the soul, I would be attending the medical conference in Chicago after all. I was excited, mainly because it would be my first time being that far from home without my parents. It was a two-week program at the University of Chicago. I started mentally preparing, researching Chicago, O'Hare International Airport, and everything else I could learn about the city. One day, The Breakfast Club came on TV, and, realizing it was set in Chicago, I just had to watch it.

When I arrived, along with 300 or 400 other students, the organizers had signs up to welcome us. While we were there to learn about opportunities in medicine, it was also an opportunity to meet kids from all over, including all kinds of girls. I was the only student from South Carolina. My assigned roommate was a kid from Michigan named Farhan. Like me, he was shy, and we related on many levels. We quickly bonded.

Farhan is a big-time physician in Michigan now. But that program in Chicago discouraged me from going to medical school.

Our activities included sitting in on a lecture about the heart and viewing cadavers. We also heard how tough it is to get into medical school: how many people apply every year, how you need to keep your studies up and meet all these other requirements. I realized there was no way I would be able to get into something like that. I cowered down and became discouraged, because I was around all these really smart kids. I knew where I was from, and this was a whole 'nother level. Medicine wasn't the career path for me.

The time required was a major deterrent, too. Going to med school would add up to eight years of my life! But while at the conference, I also learned about pharmacy. In just six

On campus at the University of Chicago.

years, you could get your doctor of pharmacy degree and become a pharmacist. That sounded pretty good! It might be easier than getting into med school, and it was shorter. By the time I left Chicago, I had set my sights on pharmacy.

Back home in Bennettsville, I did some research and found that the University of South Carolina had a pre-pharmacy major. Everything became about pharmacy at that point. I called the USC College of Pharmacy and asked all kinds of questions about the program. When I went to USC a year later, I did so as a pre-pharmacy student.

***

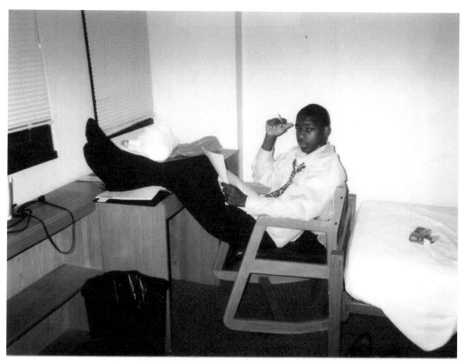

Looking over some medical school information in my room at the summer conference.

During my senior year of high school, my guidance counselor called me into her office to give me a heads-up two days before the annual awards ceremony. For being the only student in Marlboro County to attend the National Youth Leadership Forum on Medicine, I would receive an award before the whole student body.

I was OK with receiving awards as part of a group. But this would put me in the spotlight alone. I would have to walk down and receive this award by myself. My guidance counselor shouldn't have told me that! The day of the awards, I pretended to be sick and stayed home from school. My girlfriend called me on a payphone during lunch and said, "They called your name out for an award today." I hadn't told her about it. My mom also didn't find out about it until after the fact, and I didn't tell her that I had known in advance.

***

The fire that had been lit in me the previous year after I learned I wasn't a junior marshal was still burning. As a senior, I was determined to make straight A's all year and graduate with honors. I did end up making straight A's and raised my GPA to over 3.5, but I didn't graduate with honors. The selections were based on grades through March or April, and at that point, I hadn't quite made the cut.

But the fact that I made straight A's served as a testament to myself of what I could do when I got intentional. That attitude carried over into college.

Farhan and I on the last day of the National Youth Leadership Forum in Chicago.

5

PHARMACEUTICAL LETDOWN

I had taken my SAT as a junior and scored about 1000, which wasn't great, but it wasn't bad for a junior. I applied early to the University of South Carolina and found out in December of my senior year that I'd been accepted, so I didn't take the test again.

My freshman roommate at USC was Lance, my friend who had gone to Governor's School. Lance came to USC undecided on a major, while I was laser-focused on pharmacy. He ultimately chose pharmacy, too, and was accepted into pharmacy school the first time he applied—unlike me. That's when I realized what Governor's School had done for him.

Lance excelled at introductory biology and chemistry. I was good in biology, thanks to my good memory. But I struggled in chemistry and had to ask him for help at times. I also had to get tutoring to make it through that class.

In our second year, a phone call came about 6:30 one evening to let Lance know he had been accepted into pharmacy school. I answered the phone and recognized the voice on the line as the dean from pharmacy school, because I had taken to heart the advice they'd given us at orientation: stop by from time to time to make yourself recognizable.

I was happy for my friend. But I hadn't yet gotten a call—and, as it turned out, I wasn't going to get one. In the meantime, I checked my mail every day and waited for that call, not knowing how the news would arrive. When reality finally sunk in, it was a hard pill to swallow.

During that time, I never let Lance know how much it bothered me, and I was still happy for him that next year, as we moved off campus and into some apartments by the football stadium. Then classes started our junior year, and he was going off to pharmacy school while I was stuck taking a biology class. I still planned to apply to pharmacy school again in the coming cycle, and technically I was still a pre-pharmacy major, but I had started gearing my curriculum toward obtaining a biology degree. I figured this wouldn't hurt my chances since everyone pretty much takes the same courses the first two years anyway.

When it was time, I applied to pharmacy school a second time, and again I didn't make the cut. Each morning I woke up to the realization that, while my friend was learning how to become a pharmacist, I was stuck studying germination and other random biology—not what I had expected to be doing.

***

UNIVERSITY OF
SOUTHCAROLINA

February 25, 2005

Office of the Dean
College of Pharmacy

Gary Bethea

Dear Mr. Bethea:

It is my duty to inform you that the Committee on Scholastic Standings, Petitions, and Admissions of the College of Pharmacy has decided not to accept you into the professional program for the Fall, 2005 class. There were many qualified applicants, more than the College of Pharmacy could possibly accept. We urge you to re-apply next year if you have any interest in pursuing a career in pharmacy. Applications will be available online at www.cop.sc.edu beginning September, 2005.

We appreciate your interest in the College of Pharmacy. I wish you success in your future academic and career pursuits.

Sincerely,

Wayne E. Buff, Pharm.D.
Associate Dean

WEB/ew

UNIVERSITY OF SOUTH CAROLINA • COLUMBIA, SOUTH CAROLINA 29208 • 803/777-4151 • FAX 803/777-2775
An Affirmative Action / Equal Opportunity Institution

My second rejection letter from UofSC college of pharmacy. It was tough receiving this letter at the time but I have now come to see it as a blessing.

Let me backtrack for just a moment to say that college wasn't all books. Throughout my time at USC, some of my extracurricular experiences were just as formative as my academic ones.

Starting our freshman year, Lance and I spent a lot of time with my cousin Bumper and another friend named Quentin, both of whom were attending South Carolina State, about 40 miles away in Orangeburg. They'd visit us at USC, and sometimes we'd go see them at State.

Lance and I also became close with a guy named Brian who lived on the same dorm hall. To this day, he's a part of the "team."

In our sophomore year, we met Taurean, known as T, through Brian; both were mechanical engineering majors. By then, we had moved into bigger dorms, and Brian roomed with Lance and me. T would come to our room to study with Brian, and we all became close as a result. Lance, T, Brian, and I were like the four horsemen. A few others, like Marty, aka, Schoolboy; Tripp; and Jerome also would come from State for parties and to hang out. They, too, were from Bennettsville. Meek, a USC student who was dating a girl who lived in the dorm beside us, would drop by our dorm room when we were playing Madden football. He was wild, but he was our guy. All of us at USC and the guys from State became known as DA CAMP.

Quentin, Bumper, T, and I made rap music together. Nobody played an instrument, but we'd put songs to beats

I got from my brother. Otis would record us, and I'd make little videos using the camcorder my mom got me when I was sixteen. I put out a mixtape our junior year. Lance didn't rap, but he kept a book bag full of my CDs and sold about 200 of them around campus for $3 apiece. T and then Quentin followed with their own mixtapes.

Schoolboy, Quentin, and Lance back in 2006. Lance had drove to state to sell some of our mixtapes.

My frustrations about pharmacy school got channeled into my music. I rapped about my experiences with girls I was dating, school, money, and violence. The violence wasn't excessive, but I might rap about what would happen if you crossed me. But as I started growing closer to God, I started to feel convicted about certain things. I stopped rapping about things I wasn't doing. Eventually, I stopped rapping altogether.

During my freshman year at USC, I was still dating my high school girlfriend, who was a year behind me. In high school, I hadn't always been faithful, but she always believed me when I told her I was innocent. After I got to college, though, I found out she was cheating on me, and that was a blow to my pride. I largely quit talking to her; I didn't want to take her to her prom, though we were technically still together. My pride wouldn't let me fight for her. Our relationship deteriorated, and we were history by the end of my freshman year. I don't think we ever said we were going our separate ways. She just started being with the guy she had cheated on me with, and I let her go.

For quite a while, I really didn't date anybody else in college. Every girl I went out with was just a friend. I didn't want to be in a serious relationship.

***

Through all these experiences, the groundwork was being laid. There was a plan—I just couldn't see it. After arriving at USC, I had landed a job in the pharmacy school, working in the Palmetto Poison Center. I was doing all I could to be a worthy applicant, and my grades were good, but I still never got in.

Looking at my life now, I see God's wisdom. I wouldn't have been happy as a pharmacist. I had chosen pharmacy simply because it seemed easier to get into than med school and would take just six years instead of eight. And it seemed like a profession that would allow me to make some money. I remember seeing a shirt that read, "Zero to 90,000 in Six Years" and thinking: *man, I can make $90,000 in six years!* I remember seeing the guy in the CVS wearing a white coat. It was a nice, respectable job.

None of those was a valid reason. But that realization came only with hindsight.

I was in my senior year at USC, but because I had switched my major from pre-pharm to biology, I wasn't going to graduate until the following December—unlike most of my classmates, who would finish in May. That summer, I had multiple appointments with my hometown dentist, Dr. Philip Benton, to get some fillings. Dr. Benton and I had a good relationship and could talk honestly. I confessed to him that my pharmacy plans weren't working out, and he said, "You should try dentistry."

I had been interested in dentistry at one time, but it seemed a lot like med school. Again I thought, *That's eight years out of my life.* Plus, it was probably just as tough to get into the dentistry program. But he assured me it was a good profession and said he would write me a letter of recommendation. That convinced me to give it a shot.

So I got my books together for the DAT, the Dental

Admission Test, and that summer, I started studying for it while also studying to graduate. I applied to MUSC, the Medical University of South Carolina, which has the only dental program in the state. But I applied late because I didn't take the DAT until late November, and by then, the acceptance process was well underway. So to hedge my bets, I also applied to Howard University in Washington, D.C., and to Meharry Medical College in Nashville, Tennessee.

I had never heard of Meharry before another godly intervention. That summer, there was a guy in my biochemistry class who wanted to be a dentist. One day in November, as I was getting my dental application ready, I bumped into him in the BI-LO grocery store near campus, where I had gone to buy bread. As a senior with little money and a limited meal plan, I largely subsisted on peanut butter and jelly sandwiches.

He asked if I was planning to apply to Meharry. I said, "Meharry? What is that?" All I had on my mind was MUSC and Howard. He said, "You should look into Meharry. They accept a lot of African American students."

I went back to my apartment. I had a booklet that listed all the dental schools, their makeup, the average GPA of the students they accepted, and so on. And there was Meharry. At the last minute, I added it to my dental application, which I mailed in December.

Later that month, I was sitting in graduation, and to be honest, I wasn't thrilled to be graduating, because I really had no prospects. What was I going to do with my biology degree? The person sitting to my right was talking with the person in front of me; both had jobs lined up, while I had nothing. I didn't know whether I would get into one of the three dental schools I'd applied to and was hoping maybe a biology lab would hire me.

I had gone to church the whole time I was at USC. But as graduation neared and I didn't know what I was going to do, I started getting closer and closer to God. I'd stay up late at night reading my Bible, and I was going to a Bible study regularly.

(The Bible I was reading was a Life Application Bible my godmother gave me when I graduated from high school. Alma Hill, who went to my church, became my godmother during my senior year of high school. She had been looking for somebody to help, asked around, and was led to me. It was good timing for me, and that Bible proved to be a godsend at a time when I needed it.)

One day I was in the computer lab looking up jobs I could apply for with my biology degree, and I just stopped what I was doing and started praying: *God, just give me something to do. Whatever you want me to do, I'll do it. Just give me a purpose.*

February came, and the pastor at my church in Columbia preached a series on fasting. There are various biblical reasons for fasting, including drawing closer to God in prayer, seeking His guidance, and humbling yourself before

God. I decided to fast, but I had never done it and had no clue what I was doing. I just went cold turkey: not only did I stop eating, but I wasn't even drinking water. All I did was pray. I ended up getting sick. I became dehydrated and just lay in bed, trying to sleep it off. I got so bad off that my friend T took me to the emergency room, where they hooked me up to an IV and pumped fluids into me until I felt my energy coming back.

***

After I got out of the hospital, a couple of events happened that seemed relatively minor at the time.

One day, I was napping around lunchtime when my friend Meek dropped by and told me one of my taillights was busted out. We went outside to look at my car, a champagne-colored 2001 Mercury Sable with tinted windows that I had gotten my junior year and which I called the "champagne room." In addition to a busted taillight, it had scratches all over the trunk.

I had no enemies that I knew of, so I was puzzled. But I eventually discovered the culprit: a guy who was jealous that I had been talking with the girl he'd been seeing. She was living in the apartments by the football stadium, and we had met at the bus stop about five months prior. She was coming to hang out with me a lot, and I guess that had set him off. Up until that point, I had never even known the guy existed.

Right after that episode, I received a letter telling me

The Champagne Room.

I had an interview for dental school in Nashville the next month. It was a prayer answered amid the resistance the devil seemed to be throwing at me.

Having limited funds, and not trusting my car to make the trip, I took a twelve-hour bus ride to Nashville. It was twelve hours because the bus stopped everywhere! I spent the night in a hotel, had my interview, then hopped back on a bus and returned to Columbia. My first-ever trip to Nashville was a quick one.

Overall, I thought the interview went well, although one interviewer unnerved me a bit, seemingly staring at me with a mean look on his face. He'd ask me a question and then just stare. The other interviewer pointed out that, while I had gotten good grades at a good university, my DAT scores hadn't been the best. I responded that I hadn't been at my best the day of that test, but my grades showed what I could do in class. Still, I returned to Columbia thinking I wasn't going to get into Meharry.

6

A NEW DIRECTION

After graduating from USC in December 2006, I worked as a valet at the Columbia airport while taking one more class, a once-a-week physics lab, which I needed to fulfill my requirements for entering dental school. Two older guys and I took turns retrieving cars, waiting in the little valet station for people to arrive on their flights. While waiting, I'd read my Bible. Late at night, I was the only one there, and I'd read and read until my shift ended around midnight.

The news that I had been accepted into dental school arrived in March 2007 by certified letter, the kind you have to pick up at the post office. My mom received the notification at home in Bennettsville. She called to tell me about it; she was going to the post office the next day. She and I prayed on the phone about it.

That night, I dreamed I was speaking to youths at my hometown church. That was strange, because I'd always been afraid to speak in public, especially at church. I could read announcements on Youth Sunday but feared being called on to actually speak. I'd find ways to dodge it. But that dream seemed to be directing me: "You got into dental school, and you're going to speak about it." I took the message to heart. I woke up with confidence that morning, knowing I had gotten in—even before my mom called to confirm it.

I had gotten into dental school my first time applying, one of 58 students accepted out of 2,000 applications. Those were tougher odds than when I applied to USC's pharmacy school, which accepted about 90 out of 600 to 700 applicants. I couldn't credit anyone but God for what was happening in my life.

In June, I moved to Nashville to start dental school at Meharry Medical College.

**

A brief flash forward: The first time I came back home to Bennettsville from Nashville, in late November or early December, I spoke to the youth and adults at my hometown church. It was packed that Sunday. That was my first time ever speaking to students or at church. It was also the first time, other than during the trunk conversation when God assured me of His saving grace, that I received confirmation from Him about something in the future.

I was still a little nervous about speaking, but the dream had prepared me. Call it an epiphany or déjà vu in reverse. By the time I got up to speak, I realized: this is happening just like I saw it. Ever since then, I've been asked to speak here and there: at my hometown church or another church or to kids at school.

***

Despite my initial ignorance of Meharry Medical College, it is a storied institution, founded in 1876 as the South's first medical school for African Americans.

I started two months early, in an optional program called MAPS that allowed students to prepare for the heavy load they'd be facing.

When I first arrived in Nashville, I didn't have a place to stay or money for an apartment. All I had was the clothes I'd packed into my car. Campus housing wasn't available yet, because school hadn't officially started. Fortunately, a lady named Ms. Connolly, who worked in Meharry's front office, allowed me to stay in a room at her home for a month or so. I slept on the floor the first couple of nights until I got a blowup mattress.

The MAPS program allowed early dental and medical students to take a few classes together. One of those was gross anatomy. Dental students don't really have to know about the lower extremities, but we learned about them now, as a preview of the intense studying and labs that awaited us. Our first test was frighteningly difficult. Afterward, students were talking among themselves, trying to figure out how everybody else had done. Almost everybody failed; I felt bad about my 70-something until I learned that many of my peers had scored in the 50s and 60s. So that gave me a little confidence going into the start of the actual school year. These scores didn't carry over, thank goodness, but they helped get us get ready and let us meet some of our classmates. I'm so glad I participated in that program.

Right before school started, I got my own two-bedroom apartment. My mom and my godmother had sent money for a deposit. Then Ms. Connolly told me about a new student who had rented a place, sight unseen, before arriving in Nashville. When he got there, he wasn't happy with it, but it was too late to find another place. She asked if I'd be open to letting him stay in one of my two bedrooms. I was hesitant to share my place with some guy I'd never met, but I told Ms. Connolly to have him call me.

My first conversations with Jameiko were on the phone, and he had a heavy Caribbean accent. He was originally from the Turks and Caicos Islands, a British territory southeast of the Bahamas that I'd never heard of. He had come to Meharry from the Miami campus of Nova Southeastern University. After we talked, I started thinking that having someone to share the rent would be helpful, so I decided to let him move in. When I saw where he'd been living, I understood why he didn't want to stay there. I helped him move his belongings to my apartment, and we clicked from the start. For my first couple of years of dental school, he was my roommate. And he turned out to be my brother from another mother.

Jameiko proved to be a really smart guy. He was always studying: in the library, in the apartment, wherever. He'd come home and find me studying on the couch with the TV on. I started worrying that maybe I wasn't studying enough. But when we took our first round of tests in biochemistry and gross anatomy, I had some of the highest grades in the class. After that, Jameiko joked that I could study for about ten minutes and be good. It became a running joke.

He was amazed by how well I was doing academically. He was great too, and he really excelled with his hands. This didn't become immediately apparent, because the first part of dental school was basically just academics. You didn't get into the hard dental requirements, like cutting on teeth and doing detailed drawings, until later.

As the semester went on, we got to the head-and-neck part of gross anatomy. That's the hardest part for most people, because of all the nerves and blood vessels. But when we took our first head-and-neck test, I had one of the highest grades, a 90.

Gross anatomy was the only class that med students and dental students took together. My score on the head-and-neck test made members of both groups conclude that Gary Bethea was "on" academically. Fact is, it came pretty easy. USC had prepared me well. Plus, I've always had a good memory, and to me, gross anatomy was just remembering where this nerve is, what this blood vessel connects to, etc. I just had to put the time in, study, and go over it a few times until it was locked in my brain. Biochemistry and some other classes required more from me, because calculations were involved. But in general, academics came pretty easy that first semester. After one semester, if I remember correctly, I was No. 3 in my class. A guy named Quinton Slaughter was No. 1. Quinton is now an oral surgeon in Texas.

After the first year, we had more classes in the actual dental school, not just all the general first-year classes like biochemistry and biology of diseases.

I was glad to have Jameiko as a roommate, and not just because he was such a good student. We became very close and made a lot of good memories. After one of our first tests, his girlfriend, whom he later married, brought lobsters up from Miami. He cooked them, and we celebrated. People found out we were eating lobsters and started trying to come to our apartment. I posted a picture of a lobster on social media, and that became a bit of a joke. Everybody would ask us, "Y'all got lobsters over there?"

Jameiko was somebody I could lean on during dental school. When I left South Carolina for Nashville, I pretty much left behind everybody I knew. With the exception of the quick visit for my interview, I'd never been to Nashville before. So I really didn't have anybody but my classmates, a lot of whom were in the same situation. We all became really close, because we had to get through it together. In dental school, our total class size was 55 to 60. We did everything together. You got to know everybody, and everybody depended on everybody else, because it's hard. To this day, I call on many of my classmates if I'm in their city. Years after graduation, when I proposed to my wife, one of my classmates, Harvey Spencer, helped me with my plan. That's the kind of camaraderie we had.

***

I loved Nashville from the start. During my four years there, I experienced much of the city. Ms. Connolly, whose house I stayed in, lived in the suburban Hermitage neighborhood, on the east side of Davidson County. My apartment was in Bellevue, a quiet community on the hilly west side.

From the standpoint of food, Nashville is way different from Columbia, with lots of variety. When my parents visited me in Nashville for the first time, I took them to the Pancake Pantry in Hillsboro Village, which has some of the best omelets I've ever eaten. My friends and I used to eat a lot at Monell's, a family-style restaurant in the Germantown neighborhood. Downtown was different, too, with music everywhere.

Sports fans have the NFL's Tennessee Titans. In Columbia, of course, we have the USC Gamecocks. Even when I was in Nashville studying hard and getting through dental school, I remained a big Gamecocks fan. On Saturdays during the game, I'd think about everybody back in Columbia tailgating and having a good time, and I'd start missing it.

Now I miss Nashville. I appreciated it while I was there,

but sometimes you don't appreciate a place as much as you should until you leave—just as I didn't fully appreciate Columbia until I left. But I knew I was going to move back after I finished school to be close to friends and family. It's a good place to raise a family.

Toward the end of my time in dental school, I started looking at getting into the residency in Columbia, which was one of the toughest in the country to get into.

***

One dental school professor who made a big impression on me was Dr. James Tyus, a Meharry legend who taught tooth morphology. When you start learning about the teeth, you have to understand and learn to draw each one. You learn how to wax up a tooth and how to carve a tooth. Dr. Tyus was so good at breaking it all down for us. His three-hour lectures were never boring.

Freshman year of dental school. Tooth morphology class.

Dr. Tyus loved all his students, and everybody loved him. I was amazed at how he could tell you every detail there was to know about every tooth. He also was great with his hands. When we had to start carving and doing all these other physical activities, we'd line up to ask him questions, and he patiently took his time with every student.

When I was in school, he taught Monday through Friday, practiced dentistry three days a week after work, led a male choir, and even preached some Sundays. I heard him speak on multiple occasions.

I was fortunate to work with him as an assistant during my last two years at Meharry. I'd go straight to his office after school, work a few hours, and get home around 9:00 p.m. I learned so much from watching him, not only at school but also in his dealings with patients. Dr. Tyus became my mentor. My admiration for him continues to this day. As a practicing dentist, I find myself emulating him.

He taught me so much on so many levels. He was always doing something, being purposeful with no wasted time. My wife says that about me now, that I'm always into something: working on a project, participating in a church-related event, or filming something. My days are filled—not with busywork but with actual productivity. I have learned that God doesn't call us to be busy, he calls us to be fruitful. I got that from watching Dr. Tyus.

Another influential dental professor was Dr. Roosevelt, who has since passed away. He used to get on us students, and we didn't understand that at first. He would talk junk to us, like "Back in my day, we did it like this." He always seemed to be ragging on us. But we learned a lot from Dr. Roosevelt. He'd have us students laughing at one another. He wasn't as kind and gentle and patient as Dr. Tyus, but he was one of those guys you can't forget.

Dental school was a hard four years, but it was worth it. As I said earlier, I had already been developing my relationship with God before I got to dental school, but that solidified it. You need God to get you through something like that! And though I bonded with my classmates and miss them, I wouldn't want to go through it again.

From left to right: Phillip, Antwan, Jameiko, myself, and Chris at the Meharry Carabelli Ball our sophomore year of dental school.

The challenges extended beyond the academics. One was learning indirect vision by working on a mannequin while looking in a mirror. We weren't in a real person's mouth, but we had to act as if we were. Many dentists develop back problems because they don't learn to look through the mirror and maintain the proper posture and ergonomics.

Studying for part 1 of the dental boards. At that time, part 1 was taken between your sophomore and junior year. I passed part 1 in July 2009.

After two years in the classroom, you also start spending time in the clinic with real patients. The summer before I started in the clinic, I was nervous about working on real patients. But an event that summer put things into perspective.

My cousin Romeon's girlfriend, Sherika, whom he had dated since high school, gave birth to twins. That July, right after having these babies, she died. At her funeral, I reflected on all the times I'd had with Romeon and Sherika, including the double dates my girlfriend (Sherika's cousin) and I had been on with them, and seeing his pain made me think about how serious life is. These children were going to grow up without their mother. It reminded me of my own mortality, and suddenly, going back to dental school and working on patients seemed so small. Why was I afraid? This was something I signed up for, was called to do, was ready to do. My fear evaporated.

Still, to go from learning on a mannequin to working on our first patient was daunting. We had gotten a taste of it when we had to practice giving each other shots. One classmate was so afraid of messing up that he briefly blacked out. When it came time to put anesthetic in a syringe and numb a fellow student, everybody had the shakes! We got used to it, but when doing it for the first time in dental school, we were under the microscope, with instructors checking our every step.

We had all these requirements to fulfill before graduating: X number of teeth to pull, fillings to do, root canals to perform. Starting that third year, we were on the clock.

Jameiko had the necessary hustle. He completed his requirements in December of our senior year. He did what he needed to do and did it well. One day, he did four crowns in one morning, while most students did one. He wound up graduating No. 2 in our class.

***

Remember the girl whose ex-boyfriend trashed my car in Columbia? For much of my time at Meharry, I was dating her. In the immediate aftermath of the car trashing, I stopped talking to her. She started pledging a sorority at USC, and we fell off each other's radars. Then, after I was accepted into dental school, she left a note on my car saying she missed me. We ended up friends again, although I was preparing to move to Nashville.

She managed to always be around when I returned to Columbia for summer break or Christmas. Then she started driving to Nashville to see me. She was persistent! This girl really likes me, I thought, and so I started taking her seriously. In 2008, during Christmas break of my second year in dental school, I made her my girlfriend.

She soon moved to Nashville, where she had a cousin. She stayed with her cousin but would come see me almost every day. Her presence was comforting, at least in part because she was from back home, and I had known her since 2006. Then, during my junior year, she took a job back in South Carolina, and the distance took its toll. Toward the end of that academic year, I found out she'd been cheating on me. I was angry, but I didn't want to just let her go, as my pride had led me to do with my high school sweetheart. I forgave her, but when I found out she was still cheating, I stopped talking to her cold turkey.

Splitting up broke my heart, coming right before my senior year as I was trying to fulfill all my dental school requirements so I could apply for a residency. But it allowed me to focus completely on my classes and clinic work. I was determined to get back to Columbia and that residency program.

One thing that helped me get through the difficult times in dental school was the occasional visits from my friends back home. Lance, by this time a pharmacist, came to Nashville about twice a year to see me.

***

About 45 family members showed up for my graduation May 21, 2011, at the Grand Ole Opry House. With my mother being the youngest of eleven children and my dad the oldest of eight, I have a huge family, and it was a big deal for all of them to see me get my dental school diploma on my way to becoming the first doctor on either side of my family. Everybody had a good old time. It was the first trip to Nashville for many of them, and they still talk about it. They stayed at the Opryland Hotel and went to the Opry Mills mall. It was like a vacation for them, and something I'll always remember.

My first time visiting Jameiko in Turks and Caicos. He is a living legend out there.

7

STARTING A CAREER

G etting a residency was a big deal in terms of starting my career on my best foot. I took steps to increase my chances. The summer before my senior year of dental school, I returned home and dropped by the residency program office to introduce myself. I showed my face again during Thanksgiving break. All the while, I was applying for other residencies. My Columbia residency interview took place during the fall semester of 2010. In late January or early February 2011, I found out I had gotten it.

Despite Meharry's reputation, not a lot of people outside the Nashville area seemed to know about it. And I knew how hard getting that residency would be. When I interviewed, there were more than 100 applicants for six positions. Only eighteen of those got interviews, and I was one of them. Two were automatically set aside for Medical University of South Carolina graduates, which left only four slots for everybody else.

DEEPER THAN DENTISTRY

PALMETTO HEALTH
RICHLAND

Dental Education

February 2, 2011

Gary A. Bethea

Nashville, TN 37209

Dear Gary:

Congratulations! I am very pleased and excited that you matched with the GPR at Palmetto Health for the 2011-2012 training period. In order to initiate the contract process, I need for you to sign and return this letter to acknowledge your acceptance of the match results. Please return this letter as quickly as possible to Marcia Benson in the pre-addressed envelope. An additional copy is enclosed for your records. A contract will be sent at a later date from the Office of Medical Education.

So you can plan for the start of the residency, please note the hospital has a mandatory orientation for all incoming residents. This will be held during the last full week in June. **You must attend all parts of this orientation.** You will receive information from Margie Bodie regarding the hospital orientation and several other items of importance very soon. You will also receive information about our departmental orientation at a later date.

The Office of Medical Education will also supply you with information regarding housing opportunities in the area and other materials to assist you in your transition to Columbia. Please let us know of anything we can do to help. The current residents are a good source of information about this subject.

Again, I look forward to having you with us. Should you have any questions or need further information, please feel free to contact me.

Sincerely,

James W. Curtis, Jr., DMD, ABGD, MAGD

I accept the results of the Postdoctoral Dental Matching Program and the position offered in the Dental General Practice Residency at Palmetto Health Richland from July 1, 2011 through June 30, 2012.

_____   _____
Gary A. Bethea   Date

10 Richland Medical Park   PHONE (803) 434-6367
Columbia, SC 29203   FAX   (803) 434-6299   palmettohealth.org

The interviews, before a panel of six or seven Columbia-area dentists, were terrifying. One thing they asked me to talk about was a current event that had affected me. I couldn't really think of one, so I talked about where I was from and how that affected me: coming from a small town, not knowing any dentists who looked like me growing up, and some of the things I had been through. I didn't delve into the kidnapping story, but I told them: "It's almost a miracle I'm sitting here with you all right now." I think that took it from strictly an academic issue to something that spoke to their hearts.

A couple of years after my residency, I saw one of the dentists from the panel at a restaurant in downtown Columbia, and he told me that Dr. James Curtis, program director at Palmetto Health Richland Hospital, had pushed hard for me. Dr. Curtis, who's one of the smartest dentists I've ever met, used to practice in Bennettsville, so he knew what I came from. It was gratifying to realize that he had vouched for me.

***

Within five days after graduation on May 21, I had packed up all my belongings in Nashville and moved back to Columbia. All medical and dental residencies start July 1 and run through June 30 of the next year. Mine was with Palmetto Health Richland (now Prisma).

Lance was now working as a pharmacist for CVS and doing well. He had bought a house, and he let me stay with

This picture was taken when I first moved in with Lance after moving back from Nashville. I have known Lance since our second grade class together. From the playground to the medical field. Photo credit: Jerome Pearson

him during my residency. He told me I didn't have to pay rent, but I was getting paid for my residency, so I'd give him money every month. I stayed with Lance until March 2012, a couple of months before the end of my residency, and then moved into a condo downtown.

The general practice residency, or GPR, was the right one for me. I didn't want to specialize as an orthodontist, endodontist, or oral surgeon. I wanted to be a general dentist, but a little more advanced.

I quickly realized I still had a lot to learn. When you go straight from school into practicing, it can take years to build confidence in all you need to do. To meet your dental school requirements in oral surgery, you have to pull only 20 to 30 teeth. That's really not enough to make you super confident about taking out teeth. And while you learn about implants in dental school, you don't get any experience placing them.

In my residency at the hospital, I dealt with five other new dentists, all from different places. Among the new skills we learned was IV sedation: how to put an IV in an arm and sedate a patient so you can take out wisdom teeth. Leaving Lance's house each morning on my way to the hospital, I'd pray: "God, don't let me harm anybody." Once I'd been at it a while, I started feeling comfortable. The others were learning just as I was.

My co-residents used to joke with me about how the women at the hospital were always hitting on me.

To this date, I'm the last African American male to be in the highly competitive Palmetto program. I think there was one a few years before me, and some African American females have come through after me.

Residents learn valuable skills. In addition to learning IV sedation, I was able to place a lot of implants. I got paid about $48,000 for that year (some residencies are unpaid). These factors added up to a great program.

Dr. Curtis, Dr. David Hicklin, and Dr. John Burton played a big role in helping me become the dentist I am right now. Dental school taught me a lot, but that residency took me to a different level of confidence and surgery skills.

The all-around skills I learned in that program gave me the confidence I needed when I later decided to open my own office, and to grow it as quickly as I have.

At this writing, if you look up the dental residency program for Prisma online, you'll see my face. The photo has been up there since 2012. I like to tell myself I'm sort of the face of the program!

***

While learning as much as you can during residency, you also have to think about what's next: lining up a job. In October or November, they took us to dental meetings in the Greater Columbia Dental Association. We got to network with numerous dentists, some of whom were looking to hire. But December arrived, and I still hadn't found a job.

At the children's clinic, I was told about a dentist who was looking for an associate dentist, and I reached out to her. I knew I wanted to stay around Columbia. I didn't think small, rural Bennettsville was the place to start a practice straight out of residency.

This doctor and I started talking, and I told her one of the things I most wanted was a mentor I could start working with and learning from, and maybe become a partner someday. She was looking for someone to do that, she said. But around May, as my residency wound down, the job under discussion shifted from full time to part time. Still, it was a job, so I accepted it.

Meanwhile, during my residency, I had worked with Richland Adult Dental Clinic and developed a good relationship with the people there, and they offered me a part-time job. So I was able to continue assisting that program while supplementing my income.

Despite my disappointment by the switch in hours, the first job started well. I established a good relationship with the doctor and her team, working three days a week. The practice was steady for her, but I wasn't all that busy starting out. During my downtime, I'd be in the office the doctor and I shared, trying to grow my patient base. Her patients were her patients; mine were new patients who came to the office, or people I told to come there.

I still felt the need for a mentor to help me develop confidence. This job wasn't quite the mentorship I had envisioned. While the doctor taught me things, it was not a good economical situation. I also discovered I was getting paid on collections rather than production, which turned out to be significantly less than I'd expected. In addition, I was an independent contractor rather than an employee, which meant no taxes were withheld from my paycheck; I was responsible for paying those, at the higher self-employment rate, plus my own lab fees and bills. It all added up to a rather rude awakening. Chalk it up to rookie naiveté.

Still, I was finally a dentist, and I had acquaintances in Columbia who would come to me.

One financial mistake I made was buying a used but new Mercedes-Benz. As a young African American man from Bennettsville, South Carolina, I had been anticipating the day I got to this point. But I was still paying off my student loans and paying my own lab bills, and I wasn't well versed in taxes. When tax time rolled around, I owed so much money!

Meanwhile, my Bible kept me in good spirits. That doesn't mean I was always living like a saint, but even while enjoying the single life, I went to church and studied the Word—I just didn't always apply it like I should.

Once I came to the conclusion that my first real dentist job wasn't working out too well, the doctor and I sat down and talked. She was wanting me to be more productive, but I didn't really know how to do more than I was doing. I needed her to be the mentor that I asked her about before signing on to work with her.

After a couple of years, in 2014, I decided to look for something else. I gave my employer a three-month notice. Initially, she seemed cool with that, but our relationship soon deteriorated, and she asked me to leave before the three months ended. That hurt, because I honestly felt I had done everything the right way.

That abrupt end forced me to take a job with a corporate dental practice until I could find another job with a private practice, which was my preference. I continued to work part time at the Richland Adult Dental Clinic.

Meanwhile, I was contacted by Dr. Noble Cooper Jr., a dentist who had reached out to me during my residency. I hadn't followed up with him then, because I was already in conversations with the previous dentist. Fortunately, Dr. Cooper said he could still use me. So I started working with him part time while also working at the corporate practice, and I gave up working at the clinic, because there wasn't room in my schedule. Dr. Cooper was my safety net when I needed a job, and he remains a mentor to this day. He and I would have Bible study in his office between patients. I stopped working for him right before the coronavirus pandemic hit in early 2020.

At the corporate spot, they were impressed that I could do root canals, extract wisdom teeth, and more, so they began adding work to my schedule. I was also helping the other dentists, often bailing them out when, say, a tooth would break off during extraction. I was bringing more money into the company, but I knew I couldn't stay there too long. God took care of me. When I found another job and told the corporate practice I was leaving, they didn't require me to give the typical 90-day notice, and they didn't dock my pay.

I then went to work for Dr. Arian Ray in Sumter, South Carolina. For the next six years, I commuted between Columbia and Sumter, about a one-hour drive. I worked at Dr. Ray's office for most of the day on Mondays, Wednesdays, Thursdays, and Fridays, while helping Dr. Cooper in Columbia on Tuesdays.

Working for Dr. Ray was the situation I'd hoped to find after dental school. It was him and his father initially, but his father retired a few years after I started working there. Dr. Ray and his wife, who was his office manager, treated me right. I didn't have to pay my own lab fees. I saw a lot of patients. People in Sumter came to love me. Going to work was a pleasure, and I continued to learn. I got to do IV sedation again, along with a lot of other things I hadn't gotten to do at the job that ended so badly.

I stayed with Dr. Ray for five years. Even after I'd opened my own office, I worked with him a couple of days a week until February 2019.

***

When I was living at the condo downtown, finishing my residency and then going to work for real, my only responsibilities were being in the office from 8:00 a.m. to

5:00 p.m. and paying off my student loans. I was loving the single life: dating various women, hanging out with friends, and traveling. I didn't feel the need to be committed to anybody at that point.

But dating was taking up too much of my time. During the week, I'd work all day and come home tired. When the weekend came, I divided my time among friends and women, sometimes hanging out with one person during the day and somebody else that night. It got to be exhausting.

Then I met Shayla Lites.

I first met Shayla not long after I came back to Columbia and was staying with Lance. One night, I went with him to a party in Charlotte on a party bus, and Shayla was there, though I didn't talk to her much that night. She ended up reaching out to me a year later, and we started talking. She came to see me one day at Lance's house. From then on, we were friends. I still had different female friends, because I didn't want to be in a serious relationship. After the way the last relationship had ended, I didn't have a lot of trust in women, and I was enjoying my freedom.

Shayla stood out. She seemed so different from other women I'd spent time with. For starters, she had a son. She was in pharmacy school. She was extremely intelligent. Beyond that, she was really mature in her dealings with me. Other women always seemed to be looking for me to entertain them. That wasn't the case with Shayla.

Once I was low on soap and random needs because I

hadn't gone to the grocery store. I left Shayla at my condo because I had to be somewhere. When I returned, I found she had gotten me soap and put food in my refrigerator and freezer. Things like that made me look at Shayla in a different light. She didn't expect me to take care of her. In a way, she was taking care of me (not that I was looking for anyone to take care of me).

One thing that made Shayla stand out was a little intimidating. I had never imagined getting involved with someone who had a child. Keon's father had died when he was about two years old, and Shayla was raising him by herself while making straight A's in pharmacy school. She ended up graduating No. 1 in her class, and I was blown away by how she was doing all of this.

Despite my misgivings, I realized that if I was going to date Shayla, I had to accept her child. By this time, I was being asked to speak to groups of young men, a lot of them kids from

Keon at 4 years old.

single-parent homes who needed a bit of inspiration and encouragement. Yet I was hesitant to help this young fatherless boy the way I was helping these other young people. How hypocritical would it be to stay away from this amazing woman because she had a kid? Everything else checked out: she was beautiful, smart, mature, and just different, and I was definitely interested in her. So I decided I couldn't let her child be the reason I wasn't with her.

As I started getting to know Keon, she brought him around a little more. Then it became easy. He was a cool little kid: obedient, smart, and fun to be around. Before long, Shayla and I were in a relationship, and I stopped talking to other girls. This was in 2013. I moved from my downtown condo and into an apartment. Shayla was still living in Charleston.

In February 2014, she had a month-long externship in Hawaii during her last year of pharmacy school. I flew out for a week around Valentine's Day. Some of our friends thought I was ready to propose, but, frankly, I went because she was in Hawaii with a place where I could stay for free. Once I got back home, however, I did think about it: could I marry this woman? It didn't take long to realize I absolutely could; in fact, I wanted to spend the rest of my life with her. And so that April, I proposed.

On a getaway to Nashville, I took her to the Opryland Hotel for the first time. We were on the delta riverboat cruise, which winds through indoor gardens in the hotel

Shayla and I in Maui. I flew out to see her for Valentines Day. Picture taken February 2014.

atrium, when I proposed. I had arranged for hotel staff to put up signs along the river route: Will... You... Marry... Me? At "Me," our host handed me the microphone, and I stood and proposed. Everybody else on the boat started clapping and cheering, and Shayla started crying and said yes. It was beautiful. I wish I had it on video.

We got married a year later: April 25, 2015. We had bought a house six months earlier. And that's where we plan to stay. We have a house big enough for a growing family, and unless the Lord tells me to go somewhere else, we don't plan to move again. I hate moving with a passion.

***

I proposed to Shayla on a boat ride while hundreds of bystanders watched and applauded.

It had been a whirlwind series of events since I started working for Dr. Ray. Building a patient base, saving for a ring, buying a ring, planning a wedding, buying a house, getting married. Everything was moving so quickly. The September after our wedding, we found out we were expecting, and on June 9, 2016, we had our first child together, a boy we named Gaius.

Through all these changes, Dr. Ray's office was a comfortable place to be. Life was good. But sometime around 2017, I realized I was becoming a little too comfortable. I was driven by my life outside of work, but not so much at Dr. Ray's. I loved my patients, and they loved me, but my workday wasn't really motivating me. Part of the issue was the daily one-hour commute each way between Columbia and Sumter.

I was involved in my church, and because I've always wanted to be involved in the community, I was taking time off work to speak to schoolchildren, volunteer at the children's clinic in Columbia, and so forth. My work was in Sumter, but the rest of my life was in Columbia. This was nothing against Dr. Ray, who treated me fairly, but I didn't feel that sense of community in Sumter, and I needed to be working full time in Columbia.

I was feeling the call to start my own dental practice.

It can be scary when you realize God is talking to you, or you think He might be. At least that has been my experience. I don't always understand everything God is showing me,

Shayla and I got married April 25, 2015.

but some things He starts making clear, and I can feel Him leading me toward something.

When I was at Dr. Ray's office, another dentist, Gretchen, started working there temporarily. She was starting her own office and needed to put in a couple of days of work each week while her office was coming together. We shared an office, and we'd talk when we weren't with patients or she wasn't talking on the phone about getting her own practice up and running. Our conversations planted a seed in me.

While working for Dr. Ray had been a great experience, and I had come to know the practice of dentistry—doing a root canal, extracting a tooth, and so forth—like the back of my hand, I really didn't know anything about the dental business. When it came to insurance and other aspects of running a practice, I was ignorant. Up to this point, I'd been OK with that, because having my own practice had never been my dream. But now I realized it was time to expand my knowledge rather than staying comfortable and safe. I was growing in other areas of my life, but professionally I was becoming stagnant.

God used my conversations with Gretchen to show me I needed to keep growing. The seed continued to take root after she left the office. Dr. Ray, whose father had just retired, would have liked for me to stay in his office and possibly become a partner someday. But God's plans for me didn't involve driving from Columbia to Sumter for the next

25 to 30 years.

While working for Dr. Ray, I had continued to work a couple of days a week for Dr. Cooper. He was getting older and planning to retire, and there may have been an opportunity to buy his practice from him. His office was in Columbia, where I wanted to be. And taking over an established practice with a solid patient base and cash flow in place would be much easier than starting from scratch. On the other hand, Dr. Cooper wasn't quite ready to sell for five more years or so, and I couldn't wait that long. Besides, he had built a large practice over the years, and that office seemed a little too big for me to take over. This was my internal debate.

Starting my own office would initially mean a pay cut; research has shown me that most people who start any kind of business from scratch don't pay themselves the first year or two. That would be hard to take, since I was still paying off student loans along with paying a mortgage.

But I felt God leading me to take a leap of faith. And I moved from fear to excitement, anticipation, and resolve.

Shayla' graduation from the Medical University of South Carolina's pharmacy school. She graduated #1 in her class with a perfect 4.0. Picture taken May 2014.

My dad at my mother's graduation from USC. Picture taken May 1977.

8

TAKING THE LEAP

Having moved beyond fear, I was doing everything my research told me I needed to do, talking with the people I needed to talk to, looking into the things I needed to look into, and forming a business plan.

For a while, I nervously put off telling Dr. Ray. When I finally broke the news, it was a little tough for him and his wife to take. But he understood and was happy for me.

One thing that job had afforded me was the wherewithal to travel. Shayla and I had honeymooned in Rome, and then in 2016, when she was pregnant with Gaius, we took a trip to Israel. That was an amazing trip, to be there in the Holy Land with my wife and our unborn son, visiting these historically and spiritually significant places. I got baptized in the Jordan River. Long ago, as a nine-year-old, I had accepted Jesus Christ as my Savior and been baptized, so I didn't need to do it again. But I couldn't pass up the opportunity to be baptized in the waters where Jesus Himself was baptized.

Shayla and I at the Western Wall in Jerusalem. Shayla was 5 months pregnant with Gaius.

In July 2017, Shayla, eight-year-old Keon, and I went to Zimbabwe. (Gaius, just over a year old, stayed in South Carolina with family.) The Africa trip was symbolic on more than one level. First, it would be the last trip I could afford to take for a while, because starting my own dental practice would mean a financial struggle. I was going to have to be frugal. Second, and more important, a leap was involved—literally.

At 5,604 feet across and 354 high, Victoria Falls is considered the largest waterfall in the world, with the largest sheet of falling water. It's classified as one of the seven natural wonders of the world. It's on the Zambezi River in southern Africa, on the border between Zambia to the north and Zimbabwe to the south. The Victoria Falls Bridge, which spans the river and connects the two countries, also serves as a spot for bungee jumping.

My whole life, I've been scared of things like that. I always feared drowning, and I've never been fond of heights. But before going to Africa, I contemplated what I was preparing to do in my career. And that was taking a huge leap into the great unknown, with no guarantees. As scary as that was, I knew I needed to do it. And what better way to commemorate that leap of faith than to hurl my body off a steel bridge into a 364-foot drop toward a rampaging river?

The Kololo people described Victoria Falls as "Mosi-oa-Tunya," or "the smoke that thunders." That's because of the mist from the falls and the roar of the water, which you hear

Shayla, Keon, and I at Victoria Falls.

Victoria Falls. Photo taken from the air in Livingston, Zambia.

well before you get there. It indeed sounds like thunder. Once you get on the bridge, you're so high up that, if you're like me, you feel like crawling. But I hadn't come all this way to chicken out. And so I jumped… hanging momentarily in the air before plummeting toward the river below, then swinging back up toward the bridge. When it was over, I felt a huge sense of relief that I had accomplished my mission and was back on solid ground. And I knew I could do what I was about to do.

I'll never do it again, but I am glad to have done it. Whenever I want to relive it, I can watch the video, along with so many other pivotal moments in my life that I have been able to document as an amateur videographer. That bungee jump was something I feared doing but did anyway. Similarly, I had put my fears about starting my own dental practice behind me. Once I got back from Africa, I continued my due diligence: visiting banks, comparing loans, shopping around, doing more research, talking with various people.

I started documenting on video the various steps toward opening my business. With a lawyer's help, I had registered the name Bethea Family Dentistry. I negotiated with contractors and started looking for a space. The first space I wanted was snatched up before I could make an offer.

I kept riding around, thinking about where I might locate my office. One day, I drove by a place not far from my house, and I said, "That's the spot." But I didn't have a lawyer or a realtor yet, so I made the mistake of calling the leasing agent and dealing with her on my own. I was so eager, I let the leasing agent know how much I wanted that spot. There went my bargaining power!

But the bottom line is, I couldn't be afraid of something God was leading me to do. He wouldn't let me fail. In Psalm 37, David wrote that if you delight yourself in the Lord, He will give you the desires of your heart. A lot of people think that means that whatever you want, if you delight yourself in God, He'll grant these things for you. But it doesn't mean He's going to give you everything you desire. Because our hearts are wicked, we often don't know what's best for us. The way I read that psalm, it means that if you delight yourself in the Lord, He will put the right desires, the heavenly ones, into your heart.

It hadn't been my desire to build a business from scratch. I was content doing what I was doing. But He started giving me this desire, which used to frighten me. Then it became a desire that excited me and ignited my devotion. If it was His desire for me, it was going to work. He wouldn't let it fail. That realization gave me confidence.

I had gotten a lawyer who was negotiating with the leasing agent, and they were playing hardball when they reached a stalemate. The leasing agent said somebody else was looking at the spot, and it appeared I might lose it. I started looking elsewhere. When I didn't hear from the agent for the property I really wanted, I was crushed.

During this time, an existing dental office went up for sale down the street from that office. And I started thinking about the story in Genesis when God told Abraham to offer his beloved son Isaac as a sacrifice. It was a test of Abraham's faith before God ultimately provided a ram in the bush for the sacrifice. Maybe this office was my ram in the bush: I wouldn't have to start from scratch after all, with all the sacrifice that would entail. Buying an existing practice would mean a patient base, the equipment I needed, and immediate income. So I started trying to buy this office. Bank of America approved a loan. Then somebody bought that office before I did.

Again, I was crushed. I started asking God: "What's going on? Am I being punished?" I fasted for about three days (this time without making myself sick). Not even a week later, I came across Psalm 131, which talks about David's soul being weaned. At one point, all a child knows is milk, but when it's time to be weaned, he has to go to solid food. When you take a baby away from the breast, he feels undone. He's losing all he has ever known. He may think: *what are my parents doing?*

When my son Gaius was weaned off a pacifier, I watched him crying all night in his crib. It was hard, but it needed to be done. After a couple of days, he was good. And I understood what David meant when he said his soul had been weaned. God was teaching me to trust what He already had told me.

"For who despises the day of small beginnings?" Zechariah 4:10 I was looking through the architect's plans, knowing that God is the head architect

I had told my lawyer that we needed to reach out again to the people who were leasing that first property I wanted. "I need this spot, and whatever they're asking, I'll go with it," I said. But suddenly they were reaching back out to me— with a better deal than they initially quoted! We came to an agreement, I got my contract people together, we got my permit, and on May 21, 2018—seven years to the day after I graduated from dental school—Bethea Family Dentistry opened.

Bethea Family dentistry opened May 21, 2021.

Ten days after that, on May 31, our third son, Elijah, came into the world.

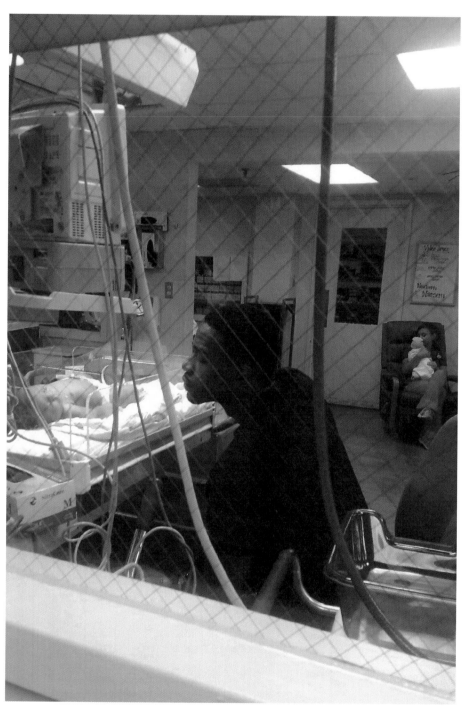

I sat here watching Gauis for hours. I remember feeling so inspired in that moment.
Picture taken June 9, 2016.

I rushed from work to get to hospital just in time to see Elijah come into the world.
Picture taken May 31, 2018.

9

THIS STORY IS STILL BEING WRITTEN

Ever since Bethea Family Dentistry opened, we've grown like wildfire, with well over 2,000 patients, mostly from word of mouth. In 2019, I was named to Columbia Business Monthly's Best & Brightest 35 and Under, and we received the BBB Business of the Year Torch Award, small-business division, from the Better Business Bureau serving Central South Carolina and Charleston. I graduated from Leadership Columbia in 2020 and was

Receiving the Better Business Bureau Small Business of the Year award was unexpected. I did not have a speech prepared so I just spoke from the heart.

selected as one of the 2020 Top Dentists in the Midlands.

While it is gratifying to be recognized for excellence in the field that God placed me in, what I do is not about awards. Our motto at Bethea Family Dentistry is "Dental Excellence Made Personal," but I use "Deeper Than Dentistry" as a hashtag for a lot of things I do, like talking to young people. It goes back to my conversation with God twenty years ago in the car trunk. That's when I realized I was going to have to live for God. Now everything I'm doing is meant to bring glory to His name. Dentistry is simply my platform for that. I'm here because God opened up all these doors for me.

In that car trunk, I made a promise to Him. It took awhile for me to start fulfilling that promise, but He has been patient with me. Now that I'm married with kids, a house, and a business, I have become more and more aware of, and focused on, what I need to get done before I'm gone.

There's a saying: don't shine so that others can see you, but so that others may see Him through you. Everything I'm doing now is focused on that. I've been trying to give back to the community. I have spoken to countless elementary and high school students. We have done a free Dental Day, which involved doing free dentistry for those without dental insurance. We've donated to many nonprofit organizations. We sold T-shirts, with all proceeds going to the Transitions homeless center, and donated $3,000. I also mentor high school and college kids who are interested in the dental field. Things like that are a big part of the Deeper Than Dentistry mission.

For a year after the office opened, I didn't pay myself a salary. Thank God I was able to continue working for Dr. Cooper, doing oral surgery on Tuesdays, until after I got my office fully running. That job allowed me to keep paying off my student loans. With the help of Shayla's pharmacist salary, we were able to keep the bills paid, and I was able to pay my tithe.

Through the grace of God, everything was taken care of. That has been an ongoing lesson for me. What you're afraid to do, or think you can't do, if God tells you to do it, then do it. When you take that leap of faith, you need only to grow some wings on the way down.

Little boy from Bennettsville, SC. Some days I wake up and I still cant believe how far God has brought me.

I didn't always have a passion for the things I have a passion for now. I wanted to be a pharmacist. Now here I am, a dentist, helping people and doing things that make me happy. It's bigger than working in people's mouths. Going to work doesn't feel like working. I'm dealing with people, getting them out of pain, giving them smiles. Now a lot of people look at me as an inspiration.

With the wisdom of hindsight, I can see God moving in my life. When he gave me the desires of my heart, He wasn't giving me what I thought I wanted. He was giving me what fulfilled His plan for my life. All these blessings came on God's schedule.

When David wrote Psalm 131, he had been anointed as king, but he hadn't yet been appointed. He had to wait until it was his time. He ran from Saul for over ten years, hiding in caves with his life on the line. The people tried to make him king early, but he waited for God's timing. And so when he wrote about his heart not being proud and his soul being weaned, that was a powerful message.

As humans, we can let praise go to our heads, and pride has been the downfall of a lot of people. But we have to remember that the glory belongs to God. The more you remember that, the more God knows that you're going to bring Him glory, and He'll continue to do good things for you.

***

As the business has grown, so has the family. Elijah was

born ten days after the office opened. His impending birth gave me motivation during a tough and busy time. When Shayla was pregnant with him, I was also pregnant with the idea of Bethea Family Dentistry. He's the same age as my practice. Two babies at the same time!

Being allowed to have children is truly a gift from God. I thank Him every day for my beautiful family.

Shayla plays a vital role in everything I do. I couldn't do it without her. Like any couple, when we first got married, we were learning to coexist, juggling responsibilities and expectations. Also, I started marriage as a father, with Keon already in the picture, so Shayla and I didn't have a lot of time to ourselves. But I learned a lot in that process—lessons that have served me well as the family has grown. And while we still have a lot of growing to do as a married couple, we've found what works for us.

She lets me be the head of the household. That doesn't mean I dominate everything. We make decisions together. But she trusts me to lead the family, and she keeps me from having to worry about stuff on the home front.

The importance of a good partner in the home became increasingly evident when I was starting my business. I had so much to learn. Shayla understood, and she took up the mantle of making sure certain things were taken care of. She's the definition of what I hoped for in a wife: she just sees and knows. Her help extends to my work and ministry.

I've already talked a bit about Keon, who is nearing twelve

Family photo taken July 2018.

at this writing. He's a good kid; when somebody tells him to do something, he does it without complaining. He's also a wonderful big brother to the two little guys, and enjoys getting down on the floor and playing with them (when he's not immersed in his games).

Our second son, Gaius, is four right now. His name comes from 3 John. In that New Testament letter, the Apostle John talks about a Gaius who became faithful to the church and was held in high esteem by all. Our Gaius is a really smart kid; I see a lot of Shayla's intellect in him. He's quite outgoing and always surprising us. Sometimes he reminds me of myself when I was that age and giving my parents trouble—I hope he grows out of that!

Elijah, going on three, is laid back, chill, and enjoying life—even when Gaius is all amped up. Neither has a care in the world, and they play together all day long. But our baby boy holds his own and doesn't let his two-years-older brother chump him out of anything. I love seeing that dynamic they have, and I look forward to seeing how they grow up together.

In October 2020, Shayla and I found out we were expecting again. Keon, Gaius, and Elijah were excited when we told them. Keon said he hoped it would be twins, and I said, "Let's not get carried away!"

***

The main thing I want for my children is that they come to know Jesus Christ. Beyond that, I want them to see what I do to provide for them. I want them to see the importance of hard work in the office, at church, and at home. They know what's important in my life as a Christian, a father, and a husband, as well as a dentist.

I have mentioned how Dr. Tyus, my professor in dental school, inspired me. There was no wasted time in his life. There's nothing wrong with downtime, but I want my kids to see that I make the most out of my whole being. I want them to see me living for God.

Of course, I wasn't always this way. So, I have to be patient with them. I was out with my friends doing something I shouldn't have been doing when I got kidnapped. At one point, I was making music I shouldn't have been making. My parents were patient with me, even when I was getting into trouble, and I need to be patient with my children.

It's hard being a parent, and it's sure not easy being a kid, especially nowadays. My purpose as a father is to help all of my children grow up to be nice, respectable young adults who love the Lord and are strong in Him. That's what I would call successfully raising them, regardless of what they do with their lives.

One thing I want Keon to always know is that I try to treat him just like I treat my two biological sons, and that I'm there for him just like I'm there for them. I can't overstate what a big lesson it was for me to accept him and his mom. I easily could have missed out on that opportunity. It proved to be a blessing, because suddenly I had this beautiful family, and it keeps growing. You might say we're taking seriously God's call to be fruitful and multiply!

***

Speaking of God's call, I've accepted that He might have greater ministry plans for me. Since I had the dream about speaking at my hometown church, I've increasingly been asked to speak to people young and old.

Pastor Stephen Masolwa at First Northeast Baptist, my church in Columbia, went out on a limb by letting me go up on the pulpit and speak numerous times, despite the fact that I'm not a preacher. Apparently he saw something in me. He never put any pressure on me. He would just ask me whether I wanted to speak on a certain Sunday. It wasn't until he was getting ready to retire, and we were in a ministry meeting, that he told me he felt I had been called to teach and to preach. When I called Pastor Masolwa one day after work and told him I was accepting that call, he shed tears on the phone with me.

After that, one of our associate ministers gave me a packet. One of the questions it asked was: "What is your focus?" At first I didn't fully understand the question. But I've come to realize that my focus is marketplace ministry. It's something I've always been doing, and I don't have to be a preacher to do it. I can continue to use my business as a platform to glorify God and do ministry. This book is part of that.

Marketplace ministry is nothing new. The Apostle Paul learned a trade, making tents, and that helped him pay his way and fund his ministry. I will soon go through some minister training at my church, though I'm not exactly sure what it will look like. The bottom line, whether I become an ordained minister or not, is this: if God is calling me to speak, I don't want to ignore His call.

Meanwhile, I'll continue ministering to people through Bethea Family Dentistry. If you check out our page on Instagram, you'll see that I don't promote the business the way many dentists do. I don't use social media to show all the smile makeovers I've done or anything like that. You won't really see a lot of teeth (not that anything is wrong with that). Instead, I show people hope and inspiration. So you see inspirational videos. You see me giving back to the community. My mission has always been deeper than dentistry.

***

As a young African American dentist, I feel an added responsibility. Race can be a particularly touchy subject these days, but the upside is that it presents opportunities to make a positive impact. When I visit a class with my white coat on, it seems to mean a lot to people—teachers as well as kids. Maybe they haven't seen a black dentist, so they're happy and inspired to see me.

Blacks make up less than 3 percent of the dental population. In Columbia, I can probably count the Black dentists on one hand. Going to Meharry, a historically Black college, made a huge difference in my life. Meharry and Howard produce more than 60 percent of the Black doctors in this country. But when you're in school with all these Black doctors and dentists, it's easy to take for granted all the greatness that surrounds you, not realizing that it won't be like that when you leave.

Because there are so few of us, it is important for those who look like me to represent the profession in the right way.

That said, I believe there's really only one race: the human race. The people who really feel like my family are my brothers and my sisters in Christ. But I also love those

The lobby area of Bethea Family Dentistry.

who are not in Christ, and I pray that they will become believers and be adopted into His family.

And I pray for healing across the racial lines that continue to divide parts of this country.

***

Through it all, I still have to ask God to continue to strengthen my faith. But at the end of the day, I remain confident in what I believe, because I know He truly has worked wonders in my life. Getting out of that car trunk wasn't an accident. Whenever I'm feeling weak, all I have to do is think about everything He has done in my life, and that helps me get right back to where I know I should be.

In Old Testament times, Abraham, Jacob, and others would make altars to commemorate things God had done in their lives. It's the same now. You can make mental altars to remind you of what God has done for you. I built an altar the night I got kidnapped. The moment I got out of that trunk is an altar in my mind. I can always go to it and remember that God saved me. I have plenty of altars I can go back in and think on, and they strengthen my faith.

That night in the trunk is when I realized what true forgiveness meant. Even now, I don't do things perfectly. This is what people who don't know Christ need to realize: you're never going to be perfect in this life. None of us ever can be. That's why we need Christ.

***

This story is still being written. I am repeatedly amazed by how far God continues to take me after I think I've done my best or reached my climax. Whenever I think I've reached the highest point I can reach, God continues to show me what He can do, and to exalt me. But he's not exalting me for my sake: He's doing it for His glory.

There's no telling what God's going to do in the future. There will undoubtedly be challenges and hard times, but I will trust Him to be with me through those and pray that He will continue to use me for good. Like Romans 8:28 says, in all things God is working for the good of those who love Him.

Please let me know if I can help you come to know Him.

Family photo taken September of 2019.